A Character Building Book™

Learning About Leadership from the Life of
George Washington

Kiki Mosher

The Rosen Publishing Group's
PowerKids Press™
New York

Published in 1996 by The Rosen Publishing Group, Inc.
29 East 21st Street, New York, NY 10010

First Edition

Book design: Erin McKenna.

Photo credits: Cover © Archive Photos; pp. 4, 7, 8, 12, 20 © The Bettmann Archive; p. 16 © UPI/Corbis-Bettmann; pp. 11, 15, 19 © Corbis-Bettmann.

Mosher, Kiki.
    Learning about leadership from the life of George Washington / by Kiki Mosher.
        p.   cm. — (A character building book)
    Includes index.
    ISBN 0-8239-2421-1
    Summary: Provides examples of leadership from the life of George Washington.
    1. Washington, George, 1732–1799—Juvenile literature. 2. Presidents—United States—Biography—Juvenile literature. 3. Generals—United States—Biography—Juvenile literature. 4. United States. Army—Biography—Juvenile literature. 5. Leadership—Juvenile literature. [1. Washington, George, 1732–1799. 2. Presidents. 3. Leadership.] I. Title. II. Series.
    E312.66.M66 1996
    973.4'1'092—dc20   96-15670
                                                                                                    CIP
                                                                                                    AC

Manufactured in the United States of America

Table of Contents

Always the First

George Washington was always a leader. One of his soldiers once described him as "first in war, first in peace, and first in the hearts of his countrymen."

No matter what the job, George always took the lead. He was born a British **subject** (SUB-jekt). He became the first **president** (PREH-zih-dent) of the United States of America. He has been called the "father of our country."

◀ *George Washington was the first president of the United States of America.*

Growing Up

George was born in 1732 to a wealthy farming family in Virginia. His father died when George was 11. George went to live with his older half brother, Lawrence, whom he adored.

Lawrence was a farmer and a soldier. He taught the British **colonists** (KOL-un-ists) of Virginia how to be **soldiers** (SOLE-jerz). At that time Virginia, like the 12 other American **colonies** (KOL-un-ees), was ruled by England.

George learned many things from his brother, Lawrence, including how to be a soldier. ▶

Becoming a Soldier

George was educated mostly by his brother, Lawrence. He also learned how to farm. Later, he became a successful land **surveyor** (ser-VAY-er). But what George really wanted to do was become a soldier.

When Lawrence died, George thought that someone should take his place training soldiers. George was only 20 years old, but the governor of Virginia saw that he was a leader. He was given the title of major. Major Washington began training soldiers.

◀ *George Washington continued to train soldiers throughout his military career.*

The First Battles

Near the British colonies was land called the Ohio country. England claimed it as part of Virginia, but France wanted it too. Major Washington's first **military** (MIL-ih-tayr-ee) mission was to tell the French they must leave Ohio. The French refused to go.

Major Washington led 200 soldiers to the Ohio country. They and other British subjects fought many battles with the French. Finally, the French soldiers fled the Ohio country. Major Washington became known as a good military leader.

Major Washington led his troops against the French soldiers in the Ohio country. ▶

Breaking Away

Many of the laws in the British colonies were made by King George III of England. The colonists did not like being ruled by England. They were especially angry when King George III introduced **taxes** (TAK-sez). Each colony sent **representatives** (rep-ree-ZEN-tah-tivz) to a meeting called the Continental Congress. The purpose of the meeting was to try to make England change the tax laws in the colonies. Major Washington was chosen to represent Virginia.

One way the colonists showed their anger about paying British taxes was by dumping British tea into Boston Harbor rather than accepting it. This rebellion was later called the "Boston Tea Party."

The Fight for Freedom

King George III refused to change the laws on taxes. In 1775, the colonists decided to fight for their freedom. They wanted an **independent** (in-dee-PEN-dint) country. The Continental Congress knew that George Washington was a good soldier and a great leader. They named him general of the Continental forces, the first American army to fight the British. General Washington did not have much time to get ready to fight. His army was not trained and did not know how to fight. It had few supplies. General Washington worked hard training his army.

General Washington's hard work paid off once he led his army into battle against the British. ▶

The Revolutionary War

The **Revolutionary** (reh-voh-LOO-shun-ayr-ee) War was the war fought to free the colonies from England. On July 4, 1776, the 13 colonies declared themselves independent. The new nation was called the United States of America. But the war was not over.

The Revolutionary War lasted for many years. Many soldiers wanted to leave the army. But General Washington persuaded them to stay. So the soldiers bravely went on, trusting that their leader would help them win.

◄ *Each year a group of men reenact how General Washington bravely led his troops to victory against the British.*

Victory

General Washington believed that the United States of America would win the war. He believed in himself and in his soldiers. That made his soldiers trust him. They lived through long, cold winters with little food and few warm clothes.

General Washington did not let his soldiers down. After 6 long years of war, he led the Continental forces to **victory** (VIK-ter-ee). England was defeated, and the new country was independent.

The original flag of the United States had 13 stars and 13 stripes, one for each state in the nation. ▶

The New Country

General Washington went back home to Virginia. Shortly after the war, representatives from each new state got together to plan a new government. Once again, George was chosen to represent Virginia. He was also chosen to lead the meeting. The new government was called a **democracy** (deh-MOK-rah-see). The people agreed to **elect** (ee-LEKT) a president. A president would not be like a king. He could only rule for a few years. He could not make laws. Everyone knew whom the people would elect for president.

◀ *George Washington was elected the first president of the United States in 1789.*

The First President

In 1789, George Washington became the first president of the United States. Americans were proud to have chosen their own leader. They were happy that they had built a free nation. And they were glad that President Washington was a great leader.

In 1793, he was elected president again. President Washington was admired by his advisors, friends, and other Americans. He is remembered today as the first great leader of the United States of America.

Glossary

colonist (KOL-un-ist) Person who settles in a new country.

colony (KOL-un-ee) Group of settlers in a new area.

democracy (deh-MOK-rah-see) System of government where the people rule by electing their leaders.

elect (ee-LEKT) To choose by voting.

independent (in-dee-PEN-dint) Country that governs itself.

military (MIL-ih-tayr-ee) Having to do with armed forces.

president (PREH-zih-dent) Elected leader of a country.

representative (rep-ree-ZEN-tah-tiv) Person who speaks for a group of people.

revolutionary (reh-voh-LOO-shun-ayr-ee) Concerning great change.

soldier (SOLE-jer) Fighter in the armed forces.

subject (SUB-jekt) Citizen.

surveyor (ser-VAY-er) Person who measures land.

tax (TAKS) Money given by the people to the government.

victory (VIK-ter-ee) Winning a fight or war.

Index